OPRAH WINFREY

A Little Golden Book® Biography

By Alliah L. Agostini

Illustrated by Tara Nicole Whitaker

🌀 A GOLDEN BOOK • NEW YORK

Text copyright © 2023 by Alliah L. Agostini
Cover art and interior illustrations copyright © 2023 by Tara Nicole Whitaker
All rights reserved. Published in the United States by Golden Books, an imprint of Random House
Children's Books, a division of Penguin Random House LLC, 1745 Broadway, New York, NY
10019. Golden Books, A Golden Book, A Little Golden Book, the G colophon, and the distinctive
gold spine are registered trademarks of Penguin Random House LLC.
rhcbooks.com
Educators and librarians, for a variety of teaching tools, v̇
Library of Congress Control Numbė
ISBN 978-0-593-64525-3 (trade) — ISBN 97̇
Printed in the United States ȯ
10 9 8 7 6 5 4 3 2

D1707224

Oprah Gail Winfrey was born on January 29, 1954, in Kosciusko, Mississippi. Her mother, Vernita, named her Orpah, but people kept calling her O*pr*ah. The name stuck.

When Oprah was very young, Vernita moved to Milwaukee, Wisconsin, to find better-paying work. Oprah stayed with her grandparents on their farm. She ate fresh vegetables and made friends with the chickens.

Oprah's grandmother taught her to read when she was only three years old. Oprah loved books. They showed her a world outside her Mississippi farm. Soon she was giving speeches and reciting Bible verses at church.

On the first day of kindergarten, Oprah realized she knew a lot more than the other children in her class. Oprah wrote her teacher a note. It said, "I do not belong here because I know a lot of big words."

They moved her to the first grade.

When Oprah got a little older, she lived
with her mother and younger half siblings in
Milwaukee. They didn't have much money, and
life there was hard.

One Christmas, some nuns came to her house
and gave her and her family food and toys. The
nuns made Oprah feel special. She decided she
would help others like that someday, too.

Oprah's high grades helped her become one
of the first Black students to attend a school in
the wealthy part of town. But Oprah soon started
misbehaving. So in high school, Oprah went to
live with her father, Vernon, and her stepmother,
Zelma, in Nashville, Tennessee.

Life was different there. Vernon was strict and made sure Oprah did well in school. She followed her dad's rules, worked hard, and made many friends.

At seventeen, Oprah won the Miss Fire Prevention beauty pageant. When she picked up her prize at a Nashville radio station, a DJ heard her speak. He knew her voice was special, and he hired Oprah to read the news as an after-school job. She loved reading out loud, and now she was being paid to do it!

In 1971, Oprah went to Tennessee State University. Two years later—while still in college—she became a news anchor on television. She was Nashville's first Black female news anchor, and at just nineteen years old, she was also the youngest! Oprah presented the ten o'clock news, but her father still made sure she was home by eleven.

NEWS

Though Oprah was near graduation, she decided to leave college for a job as a reporter and news anchor in Baltimore, Maryland.

One day, there was a snowstorm. A production assistant named Gayle King couldn't get home safely, so she stayed at Oprah's apartment. They instantly became best friends.

Oprah was an excellent news anchor, but she didn't hide her feelings. Sometimes when a story was sad, she would cry. Her boss didn't like that.

But a new boss realized Oprah's emotions were a good thing—she could connect with others. He made her cohost of a talk show called *People Are Talking*. Audiences loved Oprah!

Just a few years later, Oprah moved to Illinois and became the host of her own talk show called *AM Chicago*. Again, Oprah was a hit!

One fan was a producer named Quincy Jones. He asked her to act in his movie *The Color Purple*. As a child, Oprah had admired beautiful Black performers like Sidney Poitier and Diahann Carroll, so this was a dream! She played the role of Sofia so well she was nominated for an Academy Award.

In 1986, *The Oprah Winfrey Show*, as *AM Chicago* was now called, was shown across America! That same year, Oprah started Harpo Productions (Harpo is Oprah spelled backward) and became the first Black woman to own a TV studio.

Oprah worked hard to make her show great. She talked with regular people and famous people. She had fun road trips and awesome rock concerts. She also shared secrets about herself. Her show was so popular because Oprah made *everybody* feel special.

Oprah was famous, just as she had dreamed. But not everyone was nice to her. Sometimes people made up stories about her past or said unkind things about how she looked.

Thankfully, Oprah has people she can trust, including her best friend, Gayle, and her partner, Stedman Graham.

Oprah's fans trust her opinion on just about everything. Oprah loves reading, so she started a book club. Many of the books she recommends become bestsellers because so many people want to read what she's reading.

Some fans even wanted her to run for president! Oprah wasn't interested in that job, but she spoke highly of someone who was: a rising politician named Barack Obama.

People listened. Obama was elected president twice.

Oprah's hard work has earned her a lot of money, and her big heart has led her to share her wealth in many ways. Once she gave an entire audience brand-new cars!

Education is very important to her, so she has given millions of dollars to help start and support schools. In 2007, she opened the Oprah Winfrey Leadership Academy for Girls in South Africa. The students there are all very smart girls from families without much money, just like Oprah was.

In 2011, after twenty-five years and 4,561 episodes, Oprah ended her beloved talk show. But she's still as busy as ever. She continues to interview celebrities, produce and star in movies, oversee her media platform *Oprah Daily,* run her television network (OWN), and support numerous charities.

When she's not working, Oprah enjoys
spending time with her family and friends at
her beautiful homes, taking long walks with her
"fur children" (she's had more than twenty dogs
throughout the years!), and curling up with
a good book.

Oprah never forgot how special she felt when those nuns helped her family so many years ago. Now she uses her gifts to help make millions of other people feel special, too.